Data analytics:

The Ultimate Beginner's Guide

Lee Maxwell

© 2016

TABLE OF CONTENT

Introduction

I want to thank you and congratulate you for downloading the book, *"Data analytics: The Ultimate Beginner's Guide"*.

This book contains proven steps and strategies on how to Use Data analytics: The Ultimate Beginner's Guide. Data analysis is a process of searching for information that could be used to predict, understand, or support the courses of action taken by businesses.

Taking information as it is, studying it to draw a conclusion, using it as a basis for making decisions in the business world are all part of the science of data analytics. Data analytics is one technique under data analysis and is divided into several general parts, namely: confirmatory data analysis (CDA), qualitative data analysis (QDA), and the exploratory data analysis.

CDA also known as statistical hypothesis testing is used in arriving to decisions based on the outcomes of experiments. It tests a current statistic or theory and either makes it significant or insignificant.

EDA is in contrast with CDA. Its approach is descriptive - without preconceptions. Unlike the confirmatory data analysis, the exploratory data analysis derives a theory or hypotheses based on what is found in the research. The *q*uestions to be answered usually arise from the data gathered unlike CDA where there are already a set of questions needing specific answers.

QDA is the process of analyzing data from different angles, aspects, focuses or perspectives. For instance, two people may be looking at the same thing but have totally different thoughts about it. This concept applies to QDA. How the data will be interpreted would depend on the purpose. Qualitative data analysis focuses on information that cannot be contained in numbers but in what can be deduced from images, videos, people watching, behaviours, and so on.

That said, some might confuse data analytics with data mining, when both are *q*uite different. As data analytics focuses on what is already known and seen, data mining digs deeper to find other patterns and connections not yet discovered.

Thanks again for downloading this book, I hope you enjoy it!

Chapter 1

Data Analytics

Data analysis is a process of searching for information that could be used to predict, understand, or support the courses of action taken by businesses.

Taking information as it is, studying it to draw a conclusion, using it as a basis for making decisions in the business world are all part of the science of data analytics. Data analytics is one technique under data analysis and is divided into several general parts, namely: confirmatory data analysis (CDA), *q*ualitative data analysis (QDA), and the exploratory data analysis.

CDA also known as statistical hypothesis testing is used in arriving to decisions based on the outcomes of experiments. It tests a current statistic or theory and either makes it significant or insignificant.

EDA is in contrast with CDA. Its approach is descriptive - without preconceptions. Unlike the confirmatory data analysis, the exploratory data analysis derives a theory or hypotheses based on what is found in the research. The questions to be answered usually arise from the data gathered unlike CDA where there are already a set of questions needing specific answers.

QDA is the process of analyzing data from different angles, aspects, focuses or perspectives. For instance, two people may be looking at the same thing but have totally different thoughts about it. This concept applies to QDA. How the data will be interpreted would depend on the purpose. Qualitative data analysis focuses on information that cannot be contained in numbers but in what can be deduced from images, videos, people watching, behaviours, and so on.

That said, some might confuse data analytics with data mining, when both are quite different. As data analytics focuses on what is already known and seen, data mining digs deeper to find other patterns and connections not yet discovered.

Various businesses are investing in data analytics because it has already proven its necessity in the world of trade. It doesn't matter if it's about buying or selling goods or services, the business world is intertwined with data analytics.

To put it simply, data analytics is a systematic way to understand information at hand, and use it to further business ventures. It helps companies decide what the next step would be and if that step would take them forward, or not. It has come a long way in the years that have passed and due to technology; data analytics is faster and more efficient. With the use of computers, and other kinds of modern equipment, more can be accomplished in shorter amounts of time.

An Insight Into What Is Data Analytics?

What is Data Analytics? The simplest definition of analytics is "the science of analysis." However, a practical definition would be how an entity, e.g., a business, arrives at an optimal or realistic decision based on existing data. Business managers may choose to make decisions based on past experiences or rules of thumb, or there might be other qualitative aspects to decision making, but unless data is considered, it would not be an analytical decision-making process.

Analytics have been used in business since the time management exercises that were initiated by Frederick Winslow Taylor in the late 19th century. Henry Ford measured pacing of the assembly line, thus revolutionizing manufacturing. But analytics began to command more attention in the late 1960s when computers were used in decision support systems. Since then, analytics have evolved with the development of enterprise resource planning (ERP) systems, data warehouses, and a wide variety of other hardware and software tools and applications

Today, businesses of all sizes use analytics. For example, if you ask my fruit vendor why he stopped servicing our road he will tell you that we try to bargain a lot and hence he loses money, but on the street next to mine he has some great customers for whom he provides excellent service. This is the heart of analytics. Our fruit vendor TESTED servicing my street and realized that he is losing money - within one month he stopped servicing us, and even if we ask him, he will not show up. How many businesses today know who their MOST PROFITABLE CUSTOMERS are? Do they know who their MOST COST GENERATING customers are? And given the knowledge of most profitable customers, how should you target your efforts to ACQUIRE the MOST PROFITABLE customers?

Large business uses analytics to drive the entire organizational strategy. Some examples include:

• Capital One, a credit card company in the U.S., uses analytics to differentiate customers based on credit risk and they match customer characteristics with appropriate product offerings.

- Harrah's Casino, another U.S. company, identified that against popular belief, their most profitable customers are the ones playing slots. To leverage this insight, they have created marketing programs to attract and retain their MOST PROFITABLE CUSTOMERS.

- Netflicks, online movie service, identifies the most logical movies to recommend based on past behaviour. This model has increased their sales because the movie choices are based on customers' preferences and therefore the experience is customized to each individual.

Common applications of analytics include the study of business data using statistical analysis to discover and understand historical patterns with an eye to predicting and improving future business performance. Also, some people use the term to denote the use of mathematics in business. Others hold that the field of analytics includes the use of operations research, statistics and probability;

however it would be erroneous to limit the field of analytics to only statistics and mathematics.

An Insight Into Big Data Analytics Using Hadoop

The large heap of data generated everyday is giving rise to the Big Data and a proper analysis of this data is getting the necessity for every organization. Hadoop, serves as a savior for Big Data Analytics and assists the organizations to manage the data effectively.

Chapter 2

Big Data Analytics

The process of gathering, regulating and analyzing the huge amount of data is called the Big Data Analytics. Under this process, different patterns and other helpful information is derived that helps the enterprises in identifying the factors that boost up the profits.

What is it required?

For analyzing the large heap of data, this process turns very helpful, as it makes use of the specialized software tools. The application also helps in giving the predictive analysis, data optimization, and text mining details. Hence, it needs some high-performance analytics.

The processes consist of functions that are highly integrated and provides the analytics that promise high-performance. When an enterprise uses the tools and the software, it gets an idea about making the apt decisions for the businesses. The relevant data is analyzed and studied to know the market trends.

What Challenges Does it Face?

Numerous organizations get through various challenges; the reason behind is the large number of data saved in various formats, namely structured and unstructured forms. Also the sources differ, as the data is gathered from different sections of the organization.

Therefore, breaking down the data that is stored in different places or at different systems, is one of the challenging tasks. Another challenge is to sort the unstructured data in the way that it becomes as easily available as the accessibility of structured data.

How is it used in Recent Days?

The breaking down of data into small chunks helps the business to a high extent and helps in the transformation and achieving growth. The analysis also helps the researchers to analyze the human behavior and the trend of responses toward particular activity, decoding innumerable human DNA combinations, predict the terrorists plan for any attack by studying the previous trends, and studying the different genes that are responsible for specific diseases.

Benefits of Big Data Analytics:

There are three classifications under which the benefits can be divided:

Cost Savings: The software helps the business in storing the massive amount of data and getting rid of spending the amount on the traditional database. The data is usually stored in the clusters and further transferred to the traditional database for further analysis as and when required.

Competitive advantage: The analytics help the organizations to access previously unavailable data or that data that was difficult in accessing. Hence, this increase in data access help to understand the product and work on it accordingly like planning the business strategies; hence, facing the competitive challenges.

New business offers: It helps in exploring the trending business opportunities. Many enterprises use the collected for knowing the customer trends and launching the new product ranges.

Hence, this analytics software is helping the organizations, to grow their business by boosting the sales, revenues turnovers, the marketing end results, reducing risks or improvising customer handling experience. An efficient analyst is of great importance to the organizations and learning all about its concepts can be done through a formal training of Hadoop, which is a widely chosen software, around the globe.

How Big Data Analytics Can Impact Business Results

The buzz around Big Data as with any emerging and potentially disruptive technology is only growing and enterprises are as usual wondering how to make sense of all the hype surrounding it.

What is Big Data and why is it so critical? In today's connected world, there is a surfeit of data being churned out from multiple sources, both structured and unstructured such as information from enterprise applications, social media, Internet and mobile. And the pace at which this is happening is only accelerating - it is said that the available data globally today is doubling every 12 months and is expected to only increase further.

The scale of this data has led to the apt coining of the term 'Big data.' The sheer volume and variety of data often running can be overwhelming for enterprises, which are under pressure more than ever to take informed decisions and respond in quick time. So, how can enterprises wrap their arms around this behemoth? This is where Big Data analytics steps in.

Big Data Analytics Across Industries

It is evident that enterprises need to maximize the information and knowledge that they can access to stay relevant in today's hyper-competitive environment. And here's how Big Data analytics can help across diverse scenarios. A common example is that of a retailer being able to sift through tonnes of consumer data to derive insights on shopping preferences and direct targeted campaigns. This can even be extended to capture the personal preferences and likes of the shopper and provide customized offers, leading to increased hit rates and revenues. This is a win-win situation for both parties as the consumer gets information and offers that he is interested in and the retailer enjoys revenue growth and potential customer loyalty as well. Big Data analytics does not have to adopt a big-bang approach all the time and is equally useful and effective in behind-the-scene scenarios for retailers. It can be used for a dramatic reduction in processing time when comparing product information, which resides across multiple data sources. Analyzing data allows a retailer to make intelligent decisions and helps gain a competitive edge.

Big Data analytics has immense potential in the field of healthcare too. Imagine if a hospital is able to go through its patient records and identify patterns in diseases. This can enable doctors to detect the onset of a disease much early on and the benefits of such an approach cannot be overstated. Throw in lifestyle data to gather additional insights and the possibilities are simply mind-boggling.

Obvious gains are decreased mortality rates, better quality of life due to accurate prognosis, diagnosis and treatment, and lowered insurance costs. However, the challenge will be in overcoming regulatory and patient confidentiality issues.

Another example is from the telecom industry. Mobile connections are expected to exceed 6 billion globally and in India there are close to 750 million subscribers. In this highly connected world, the amount of data available is colossal and telcos can cleverly mine this data to their advantage. The biggest impact can be experienced by studying subscriber persona and usage patterns and using that intelligence to devise targeted marketing campaigns. The analytics can also help telcos determine what additional services are likely to find favor with subscribers and offer them appropriately. This also provides opportunities to offer value-added services such as location-based services leading to better customer service.

The examples discussed give a glimpse of how Big Data analytics can help enterprises concretely and have a tangible impact on business results. However, before embarking on this path, enterprises need to evaluate their business landscape and options available that can best suit its context. This is necessary to avoid any costly missteps. As in anything else, implementation holds the key.

Chapter 3

5 Ways Data Analytics Can Help Your Business

Data analytics is the analysis of raw data in an effort to extract useful insights which can lead to better decision making in your business. In a way, it's the process of joining the dots between different sets of apparently disparate data. Along with its cousin, Big Data, it's lately become very much of a buzzword, especially in the marketing world. While it promises great things, for the majority of small businesses it can often remain something mystical and misunderstood.

While big data is something which may not be relevant to most small businesses (due to their size and limited resources), there is no reason why the principles of good DA cannot be rolled out in a smaller company. Here are 5 ways your business can benefit from data analytics.

1 - Data analytics and customer behaviour

Small businesses may believe that the intimacy and personalisation that their small size enables them to bring to their customer relationships cannot be replicated by bigger business, and that this somehow provides a point of competitive differentiation. However what we are starting to see is those larger corporations are able to replicate some of those characteristics in their relationships with customers, by using data analytics techniques to artificially create a sense of intimacy and customisation.

Indeed, most of the focus of data analytics tends to be on customer behaviour. What patterns are your customers displaying and how can that knowledge help you sell more to them, or to more of them? Anyone who's had a go at advertising on Facebook will have seen an example of this process in action, as you get to target your advertising to a specific user segment, as defined by the data that Facebook has captured on them:

geographic and demographic, areas of interest, online behaviours, etc.

For most retail businesses, point of sale data is going to be central to their data analytics exercises. A simple example might be identifying categories of shoppers (perhaps defined by frequency of shop and average spend per shop), and identifying other characteristics associated with those categories: age, day or time of shop, suburb, type of payment method, etc. This type of data can then generate better targeted marketing strategies which can better target the right shoppers with the right messages.

2 - Know where to draw the line

Just because you can better target your customers through data analytics, doesn't mean you always should. Sometimes ethical, practical or reputational concerns may cause you to reconsider acting on the information you've uncovered. For example US-based membership-only retailer Gilt Groupe took the data analytics process perhaps too far, by sending their members 'we've got your size' emails. The campaign ended up backfiring, as the company received complaints from customers for whom the thought that their body size was recorded in a database somewhere was an invasion of their privacy. Not only this, but many had since increased their size over the period of their membership, and didn't appreciate being reminded of it!

A better example of using the information well was where Gilt adjusted the frequency of emails to its members based on their age and engagement categories, in a tradeoff between seeking to increase sales from increased messaging and seeking to minimise unsubscribe rates.

3 - Customer complaints - a goldmine of actionable data

You've probably already heard the adage that customer complaints provide a goldmine of useful information. Data analytics provides a way of mining customer sentiment by methodically categorising and analysing the content and drivers of customer feedback, good or bad. The objective here is to shed light on the drivers of recurring problems encountered by your customers, and identify solutions to pre-empt them.

One of the challenges here though is that by definition, this is the kind of data that is not laid out as numbers in neat rows and columns. Rather it will tend to be a dog's breakfast of snippets of qualitative and sometimes anecdotal information, collected in a variety of formats by different people across the business - and so requires some attention before any analysis can be done with it.

4 - Rubbish in - rubbish out

Often most of the resources invested in data analytics end up focusing on cleaning up the data itself. You've probably heard of the maxim 'rubbish in rubbish out', which refers to the correlation of the quality of the raw data and the quality of the analytic insights that will come from it. In other words, the best systems and the best analysts will struggle to produce anything meaningful, if the material they are working with is has not been gathered in a methodical and consistent way. First things first: you need to get the data into shape, which means cleaning it up.

For example, a key data preparation exercise might involve taking a bunch of customer emails with praise or complaints and compiling them into a spreadsheet from which recurring themes or trends can be distilled. This need not be a time-consuming process, as it can be outsourced using crowd-sourcing websites such as Freelancer.com or Odesk.com (or if you're a larger company with a lot of on-going volume, it can be automated with an online feedback system). However, if the data is not transcribed in a consistent manner, maybe because different staff members have been involved, or field headings are unclear, what you may end up with is inaccurate complaint categories, date fields missing, etc. The quality of the insights that can be gleaned from this data will of course be impaired.

5 - Prioritise actionable insights

While it's important to remain flexible and open-minded when undertaking a data analytics project, it's also important to have some sort of strategy in place to guide you, and keep you focused on what you are trying to achieve. The reality is that there are a multitude of databases within any business, and while they may well contain the answers to all sorts of questions, the trick is to know which questions are worth asking.

All too often, it's easy to get lost in the curiosities of the data patterns, and lose focus. Just because your data is telling you that your female customers spend more per transaction than your male customers, does this lead to any action you can take to improve your business? If not, then move on. More data doesn't always lead to better decisions. One or two really pertinent and actionable insights are all you need to ensure a significant return on your investment in any data analytics activity.

Watson and the Evolution of Data Analytics and Healthcare

IBM, WellPoint and Memorial Sloan-Kettering Cancer Center are collaborating on a project using Watson as a means to develop an oncology treatment tool. Once imagined ideas regarding the progress of healthcare are quickly becoming a part of the real world. A majority of the value from Watson comes from its ability to aggregate massive amounts of medical journals. Declared a 'clinical decision support system', it will operate in collaboration with physicians and specialists.

Although it is not taking over the entire doctor patient relationship, Watson is offering valuable data driven insight for medical professionals.

Big Data analytics have been brought to the forefront of popular culture thanks to IBM's Watson. The advanced computer is a symbol of Big Data's proliferation and the future of data driven decision making in healthcare, business and government. For instance, President Obama's 2012 reelection team boasted a 100 person analytics department to analyze voters, with its own internal 12 member team to conduct analysis regarding their operations.

The beauty of Watson, rests in its ability to analyze millions of pages of journals containing unstructured natural language data in a rapid fashion. Analytics for unstructured data is the most challenging aspect of data analysis, Big Data analytics however are beginning to solve this challenge. With the progression toward electronic medical and health records, analytics will become more practical and have added use cases.

Hospitals in control of their patient data can conduct powerful analysis through technology similar to Watson, to improve future decision making. By creating a data friendly environment within an enterprise like a hospital, data will become less of a burden and more of a resource. Having the ability to assess the past 20 years of treatment in the context of real-time patient data, will undoubtedly influence future scenarios and treatment.

One instance of practical analytics usage at University of Pittsburgh Medical Center (UPMC) occurred when the new IT team used analytics to highlight patients with propensity to staph infection. Staph or MRSA is a contagious bacterium that can wreak havoc on a patient's fragile immune system and even cause death due to infection.

By conducting analytics to create a list of likely staph patients, the provider was able to specially cater to those patients in a way that prevented infection. Also applying analytics to medication procedures has the potential to drastically reduce mistakes in drug administration.

Watson is a great step forward for Big Data analytics. As the implementation of Watson within Sloan Kettering progresses, it will be exciting to see the improvements in treatment and the rate at which quality of care increases. It is highly likely that commodity versions of Watson will be made available to general practitioners within their individual practice (and eventually for consumers on their smartphone).

IBM stresses that their brain-child is much more than an advanced search engine. Its ability to process such massive amounts of unstructured data and provide contextual insight for decision makers puts it squarely in the territory of Big Data.

The Desire of US Retailers To Enhance Data Analytics

One of the most significant business trends is big data and many businesses hope to use it to their benefit today. A lot of businesses are increasingly relying on analytics and data to better understand their consumers, enhance the customer experience, and increase revenues. On the other hand, monitoring, managing and analyzing a huge amount of data can be overwhelming for the owners of a small business. This can attest that it is beneficial for a company interested in using this data to employ an outsourcing company that performs the time-consuming tasks associated with managing and interpreting analytics.

Chapter 4

Small-business owners' interest in analytics

Companies are willing to execute solutions that can help them increase their reach and better understand their target market because they are aware of the benefits that big data can give them. According to consultant KPMG's new research, merchants are driven to data management by a desire to improve client perceptions, thus increasing sales. The data showed there are many aspects in which operations utilize data and analytics to make decisions and amend company strategies. While 67 percent of merchants surveyed use analytics to revise brand and product management, 56 percent used this information to make more competitive pricing resolutions. Another 40 percent found this data useful when mounting their operations.

Businesses had opposed opinions on where data and analytics could best compel actionable insights. Fifty percent considered enhancing operational excellence would be the best possible use of data, while 36 percent believed that getting more customers would be the better use of the information they acquired.

Few firms handle data optimally

There are fairly few business owners who are well versed in managing data and analytics despite their belief of the importance that data plays in helping them grow and better serve their customers. The survey showed the following significant results based on how each company is knowledgeable on analyzing and utilizing data:

- 12 percent believe that their company has a high data analytics literacy rate

- 33 percent think that their business is moving towards a high analytics literacy rate

- 43 percent believe their firms are just average

- 11 percent admit their operations had an average-to-low literacy

While managing data isn't easy for some and may be more time-consuming for others, it still plays a vital role for a lot of businesses today. As such, companies that are unable to manage and analyze data internally may actually rely on a BPO company that can more efficiently handle the tasks. Outsourcing research can effectively analyze data, which makes it simpler for business owners to focus on developing their operations based on these insights.

Three Ways Business Data Analytics Can Improve Your Business Model

As the corporate climate becomes ever more competitive in the face of a flagging economy, companies must search out new ways to surge ahead of the opposition. Streamlining data processing and using technology to improve corporate efficiency is one way that technologically savvy organizations are maximizing their ability to compete. One of the best ways a company can use today's technology to get ahead is by employing a business data analytics program to increase their productivity and reduce errors in their day-to-day business functioning.

Here are just three of the many ways these programs can reinforce an optimal business model.

Reduce Fraud Risk

In today's world of continuously evolving technological platforms and business models, devious fraudsters have developed even more complex ways to access and defraud business through electronic channels. By using a data analytics program, savvy businesses can access several data sources simultaneously to assess patterns and trends and create "hotlists" that can be shared throughout business lines. In addition, a strong platform will allow companies to identify all fraud types, from simple acts like usage, identity and payment fraud to the highly complex business of SIM card cloning and others. Good analytics platforms will also have functions to minimize false positives and will be able to automatically flag and generate cases and manage queries and reporting.

Maximize Data Quality Management

Data quality management is at the heart of a thriving business. Many businesses, from accounting firms to retail operations, are challenged by duplicated data, redundancies and confusing entries. These types of errors can result in loss of leads, erroneous client contacts and increased downtime or an increased workforce to repair discrepancies. Using a data analytics program can clean and process data and organize this information much more time-efficiently than the usual manual database management techniques. This will free employees to pursue client leads or improve customer satisfaction and provide ease of communication and trustworthy data sharing among departments within an organization.

Manage Multiple Data Streams

Managing multiple data streams, or complex event processing, is at the forefront of the arsenal of tools for businesses that look to react quickly to changes in markets or internal issues like fraud or incorrect contact data, and increase communication between support, service and IT departments within an organization. Data can be collected on customer experience, market shifts, financial data or any combination of relevant statistics to increase operating efficiency, reduce error or miscommunication between departments or create a big-picture scenario for decision-makers in upper management to determine the course a business will take.

Strong, reliable data from multiple sources results in smarter decision-making at all levels.

Whatever your business needs, an analytics program can provide your business with a level of efficiency that can't be matched with outdated manual input systems.

Chapter 5

What Is Meant by Big Data Analytics Training?

One of the latest and advanced technology trends in vogue is the Big Data Analytics training. This stream of technological improvement concerns an advanced process of collecting, managing and analyzing a bulk amount of facts.

The term 'Big Data' refers to the kind of facts that is so vast and complex that it is difficult and cumbersome for conventional facts tools to capture, analyze or store them. In the course of its application, huge info lets analysts mark the trends, obtain insights and go for relevant predictions. Leading companies owning international acclamation such as Amazon, Walmart, and eBay have been known to deal with huge info in their operations of late.

Hence, there has been a noticeable expansion in the job scope for skilled professionals for capturing and analyzing the huge info sets.

Relevance of handling on huge info

The term 'Analytics' is a much more familiar one to us as compared to the term 'Big Data', which is a more recent coinage. The prime reason behind the emergence of Big Data Analytics training is undoubtedly the increasingly vast and cumulative volume of facts that is being generated with multiple effects each day. The giant increase in this volume of facts is pacing competently with every walk of advancement if modern technology and civilization.

Huge info exercise concerns analysis of large volumes of facts that are in the order of terabytes and petabytes. In the US stock markets, shares worth billions are traded each day. While Walmart collects petabytes of files from customer transactions every hour, over thousands of credit card transactions are made all over the world every second.

Such trends have engendered a growing requirement to provide professionals with apt handling on huge info analysis.

Numerous Professional Organizations have taken up helps to promote and provide training on Big Data analytics

Different corporations and exercise companies have reportedly set foot on propagating a wide range of certification and analysis handlings on huge info. These preparation courses are run with the objective of providing an in-depth and comprehensive overview of Huge info, how its management and analysis can be executed with professional dexterity and efficiency by using effective tools such as SAS and R language. There are also several other such user-friendly tools which enable ease of access and operation.

Prominent role of NIIT and GNIIT in providing professional preparation on Vast Data

Keeping a keen eye on the growing demand of the current hour, it has set to offer efficient handling courses to professional enthusiasts. It has taken sincere notice of the requirement of IT professionals and hence, is providing huge info handling with special attention in the area of advanced analysis.

The courses offered by NIIT's Statistics Analytics experts have been building up learners with appreciable proficiency in the concerned field, enabling them to escalate on their career path with specialized adroitness in handling huge info, which has become a prior requisite in most of the recognized organizations of today.

For those willing to build a career in the field of Business analysis, it has designed proficient handling programs in IT and Business analysis. The programs have been designed to effectively impart statistics analyzing capability to the learners so that they are confident to work exercising personal productivity tools, creative thinking and other relevant skills.

Data Analytics: Services Beyond Conventional Summarization and Records

What do you do when a carefully planned task gets the wrong way? No doubt, each one of us has experienced such a situation in our everyday lives. We simply sit back and analyze everything that has happened and try to identify the root cause of the problem. In addition, we also take into consideration the factors that could have affected the situation. This is the simplest form of analysis that we often use in our everyday lives. The same holds true for businesses who utilize data analytics solutions when faced with trouble of any kind.

Business analytics enable business owners, managers and strategic marketing professionals analyze and understand business opportunities. Not only this, analysis is also used for positioning of products in the market. As a matter of fact, business intelligence is the only one that helps a business convert heaps of raw data into useful business information that drives business decisions. It is often observed that the companies which apply data analytics outshine their counterparts. Undoubtedly, data has become a crucial resource for the top management. Well, we cannot deny the fact that the extraction of information from a database and conversion of the information into useful insight needs meticulous efforts. This is the reason business conglomerates often opt for data companies.

At present, a business is faced with pressure from all sides. Business owners need to be proactive. In addition, they should also focus on their value chain. Moreover, the dynamism of the market has compelled organizations to adapt themselves to the changing conditions. Access to data analysis and financial planning allows a business manager to seek business success beyond the conventional horizons. Data reveals valuable information and insights about a company. Tapping the latent potential of data is inevitable in a contemporary organization. Not only does data help you draw inferences on the basis of past events, but also allows you to prepare for the future. Analytical solutions deploy business intelligence techniques that are based on data mining. This facilitates the creation of powerful and feasible business solutions.

Data analysis enables companies from a variety of industries such as retail, healthcare and financial services to use disparate information and data. In addition, organizations are also provided with a deep understanding of driving factors including categories of customers, sales performance of a product, buying behavior of a customer and many other important things. Apart from all this, analysis of data also enables an organization to gain foothold in new markets. Analytics allows a business owner to gain insight into different aspects of a business. Analytical services allow organizations to plan for the future.

The services also give you the confidence to succeed in every sphere of business.

No matter whether you outsource your customer service activities to the best contact center or hire the best marketing agency, data analytics is the only magic potion that can help you stand the test of time amidst a plethora of organizations battling for the top position. So, start using analytical services as early as possible.

How-To: Data Analytics

This is a very simple post aimed at sparking interest in Data Analysis. It is by no means a complete guide, nor should it be used as complete facts or truths.

I'm going to start today by explaining the concept of ETL, why it's important, and how we're going to use it. ETL stands for Extract, Transform, and Load. While it sounds like a very simple concept, it is very important that we don't lose sight during the process of analytics and remember what our core goals are. Our core goal in data analytics is ETL. We want to extract data from a source, transform it by potentially cleaning the data up or restructuring it so that it is more easily modeled, and finally load it in a way that we can visualize or summarize it for our viewers. At the end of the day, the goal is to tell a story.

Let's get started!

But wait, what are we trying to answer? What are we trying to solve? What can we calculate and/or show in order to tell a story? Do we have the data or the means necessary to be able to tell that story? These are important questions to answer before we get started. Usually, you're an experienced user on a certain database. You have a strong understanding of the data available to you, and you know exactly how you can pull it, and modify it to fit your needs. If you don't you may need to focus on that first. The worst thing you can do, and I'm very guilty of it at times, is get so far down the ETL trail only to realize you don't have a story, or no real end game in mind.

Step 1: Define a clear goal

and map out the way you're going to succeed. Focus on every step of the process. What are we going to use to extract the data? Where are we going to extract it from? What programs am I going to use to transform the data? What am I going to do once I have all the numbers? What kind of visualizations will emphasize the results? All questions you should have answers to.

Step 2: Get Your Data (EXTRACT)

This sounds a lot easier than it actually is. If you're more of a beginner, it's going to be the hardest obstacle in your way. Depending on your use there are typically more than 1 way to extract data.

My personal preference is to use Python, which is a scripting programming language. It is very strong, and it is used heavily in the analytic world. There is a Python distribution called Anaconda that already has a lot of tools and packages included that you will want for Data Analytics. Once you've installed Anaconda, you'll need to download an IDE (integrated developer environment), which is separate from Anaconda itself, but is what interfaces with the programs itself and allows you to code. I recommend PyCharm.

Once you've downloaded all of the things necessary to extract data, you're going to have to actually extract it. Ultimately, you have to know what you're looking for in order to be able to search it and figure it out. There are a number of guides out there that will walk you more through the technicalities of this process. That is not my goal, my goal is to outline the steps necessary to analyze data.

Step 3: Play With Your Data (TRANSFORM)

There are a number of programs and ways to accomplish this. Most aren't free, and the ones that are, aren't very easy to use out of the box. This stage should ordinarily be one of the quicker stages of the process, but if you're doing your first analysis, it's likely going to take you the longest, especially if you switch product offerings. Let's go ahead and go through all of the different options that you have, starting with free (or close to it), and moving on to more expensive and infeasible options if you're a complete noob.

Qlikview - there is a free version. It is essentially the full version, the only difference is that you lose some of the enterprise functionality. If you're reading this guide, you don't need those.

Microsoft Excel - I can't really promote this software enough. If you're a student you likely already own this software. If you're not, but you don't know Excel, you should consider investing because knowing Excel is usually good enough to get a job somewhere doing something.

R/Python - These are a lot more difficult for data manipulation. If you're capable of using this software for these purposes you are absolutely not reading this guide.

Depending on the particular project you're working on there are different ways to transform your data. Text analytics is far different from other forms of analytics. Each form of analytics is its own beast, and I could probably write 10 pages in depth on each kind, the issues you run into and ways to solve them, so I will not be doing that in this particular article.

Step 4: Visualize (Load)

This step is essentially the step that involves displaying it to your user. Depending on your role in the process, this can be completely different. If there is someone that is going to dissect the data you give them, you're likely not going to create any visualizations. However, you might create models that allow the end user to look at the data and understand it a lot easier, or easier for them to manipulate. This is in my opinion the most important step regardless of what your role is in an ETL process.

Why Have Companies Across Industry Verticals Opted For Data Analytics Solutions?

Undoubtedly, analysis of data has proved to be beneficial for the companies that have used it. Not only does it help in decision-making and future forecast, but also allows us to draw inferences on the basis of past events. In addition, data analysis facilitates companies in making wise business decisions through identification of problems and development of hypothesis.

The biggest advantage of statistical analysis is an unbiased approach. It is human nature to be biased towards a point of view or thought process. Consequently, the decisions made by companies are often based on the preferences of management. However, unlike human beings, data is unbiased in its approach. This is the reason data analytics consulting is increasingly being sought after by companies across industry verticals. Statistical analysis enables an organization to make decisions on the basis of facts. Therefore, the decisions that are taken on the basis of statistical analysis are unbiased and fair. Moreover, an organization is also able to get a clear picture of the situation and makes decisions accordingly.

Over the past few years it has been observed that big data analytics solutions have changed the game for a number of companies. More and more companies are utilizing data mining techniques to filter and disseminate data. You might not agree, but consistent analysis of data allows an organization to plan for future. In addition, depending on analytical solutions implies that your organization can make the most by using latest techniques and tools.

Market survey activities have become indispensable for the majority of call centers. Every outsourced contact center carries out lead generation activities for its clients. However, the study of market is mandatory before indulging in such an activity. It goes without saying that the task of lead generation cannot be accomplished without observing the trends and demands of the market. This is exactly where the services of big data analytics companies fit into the process. The representatives of an offshore contact center share their data with call center veterans. The data is utilized for study of demographics and market condition.

Apart from all this, analysis of date is also necessary to prepare a plan of action for call center executives who would be engaged in the activity of lead generation. Often, professional call center personnel are aware of market fundamentals. This is because of their practical experience and interaction with customers on a day-to-day basis. Therefore, these personnel also offer their valuable inputs to the companies that provide data analytics solutions. Moreover, sharing of knowledge also has a positive impact on the results.

All of us agree that sky is the limit for people who want to succeed. The same applies to organizations as well. Definitely, there is no specified range or scope for an organization that wishes to make its presence felt. Moreover, a tech savvy Internet world has made the task even simpler. No matter whether you are a start-up or a leading contact center, opt for big data analytics if you need a one-stop solution for all your problems.

Data Analytics - A Primer Helping Its User in Enhancing the Business

Data analytics is now extensively using the software as a service (SaaS) model. It has already overcome all the hodge podge of the higher expenses, deployment cycles, complex upgrade processes and IT infra structure, which requires traditional on premise trade intelligence solutions. Instead, a new genre of data analytics platform has emerged, which is simple and easy to set up and is also easy to use. It delivers instant business value and corporate results. There are now more than 50 applications available on the

Internet. One can choose any of these and can thus extract maximum and effective output. One of the important advantages is that it is proficient in the CRM application. Sometimes, the status of such kind of programming is shown as the 'Excel Hell' and is popular among the online corporations. However, it is considered to be the safest and the easiest choice.

The analytic platform can be considered to be a primer, which helps its user to move from the sales force automation to the salesforce.com acceleration. One can easily manage all the unwieldy spread sheets, pivotal tables, disconnected Access database etc. Before availing any particular analytics, you should understand the basic requirements. If you are employed as a sales force administrator, you must be aware about the importance of your proficiency with respect to in built reporting and dashboard capabilities of the analytic platform. And if you are still a novice to the application procedure then you should undergo a training course in order to deeply understand the exact application of the data analytics platform.

In data analytics, there are certain tools available for advanced report designers in order to create a virtual report on transactional content. This tool is also known as enterprise reporting. They provide in built scheduling of pre-authored, pixel perfect and highly formatted reports, which may include filters or pre-built prompts, thereby making them more interactive.

How Data Analytics Can Help NGOs Fulfill Their Social Mission

NGOs, also known as non-profits here in the U.S., fulfill a very important role as they seek to accomplish social good. They are in a unique position that allows them to see social need and react to it in ways that often times have more impact than other organizations efforts could. Vault is looking to apply the science and art of measurement and data analytics to help NGOs accomplish their various missions, and we believe that if applied correctly, analytics can make a huge difference in NGO effectiveness

We've broken down the process of how to use analytics for NGOs into three categories, summarized below; we feel that it presents a systematic and practical approach to foster performance management and measurement in these organizations.

Measurement

The first hurdle that must be crossed is that of measurement, of taking the time and effort to measure work and progress and collect it in a database for further analysis and presentation. There are several reasons why it is important for an NGO to measure its efforts:

-Make sure time, effort, and money are being used where they need to be

-Gain ability to prove that you are accomplishing and fulfilling your social mission

-Gain ability to show that donor and sponsor funding is being used effectively

There are a few things to keep in mind when implementing a measurement strategy. First - it is important to not only measure the end goal, but also the incremental steps that lead up to that goal. Let's say your organization's mission is to decrease the number of diabetics within a specific demographic in your community. Measuring the % decrease in diabetes within this population over a given time period is great, but it doesn't tell the whole story. Ask yourself, what are the incremental steps leading up to the lowered diabetes rates? Perhaps one is the amount of exercise the average person in the demographic is getting on a daily basis. Perhaps another is the amount of sweets or fatty foods the average person is consuming per day. As you attack these issues that lead to diabetes, measure the improvement in these areas. Then people get the whole story of where your efforts have helped reduce each aspect of the larger problem - and you can find out which efforts are the most effective at getting rid of this problem.

Second - make sure and measure regression rates. Too often we stop the measurement once the problem is solved - once we have lowered the diabetes rate, in this case. But how many of those people, after we stopped working with them, have regressed into having diabetes? This is sometimes an alarmingly high number, and when regression rates are high, that means all the work we performed to lower the diabetes rate in the first place has gone to waste. If you see through measurement that the regression level is high, it's time to implement some strategies and efforts into keeping the solution in place - that is, not losing ground once you've attained it. It's often a lot easier to keep the problem gone than to go back and fix it again. This allows you to really fulfill your mission, in a lasting sense. It wastes less resources because you retain the ground you've gained. And donors and sponsors will be excited by the fact that you can show that your solution is a long lasting one.

Analytics

Once we have measurement strategies in place, now we have lots of data on our hands. Analytics is the process by which we extract useful intelligence from this data. There are many methods of doing this, whether it be through visual analysis techniques, statistics, predictive models, etc. (specific ways on how to do these types of analysis will be the topic of subsequent posts) Many people think that analytics is a task that is beyond their abilities, but many times even simple analysis will result in sufficient intelligence that you can use to do your work smarter.

One of the most important things to remember in doing analysis is the principle of segmentation. This means looking at the data in smaller pieces, rather than in aggregate. For instance, if you want to know who your most effective workers are, break down the data to show you the hours each worker put in, and the changes in the incremental metrics we discussed above that occurred as a result of their work. Maybe you want to know which types of donors consistently give high sums to support your work - break them down by demographics, or by income, or by age, or any other variables to get a view of what your ideal donor looks like. Then you can target more of these kinds of people in your donation campaigns.

Presentation

Not to be forgotten is the element of presentation. Once you have the data and all the analysis, you need to be able to present the intelligence you've found to others in a way that they understand, and in a way that will cause a change in their behavior. The intelligence from the analytics is there so that you can be more effective in your work; however, if no one understands it, nothing will change and it will be useless. There are a few easy guidelines to follow in presenting analytical information so that it sticks and so that people will get it:

- Relate the numbers to something people understand (Just saying the number 416 can be somewhat abstract, but if you say instead "the number of people that fit in a Boeing 747? the number becomes real and concrete)

- Only show the necessary elements of analysis to get your point across (many times you'll have to go through a lot of analysis to get a few golden nuggets of intelligence, and our tendency is to want to show off all of the work we did to get there. The problem is, the process is not important to the people you are talking to. What's important is the results and intelligence, so just focus on that.)

- Keep it simple (showing too many variables on a graph, or just plain too many graphs, causes more confusion that it does clarity)

- Relate the analysis back to what concerns your constituents (Your focus should always be on solving the problem, and the analysis is only important insofar as it helps you to do that. Focus on what solves the problem for the constituents)

Hopefully this small outline gives you a framework that you can use in thinking about how to implement analytics into your organization. In the coming posts we'll be discussing more in depth how to do each of these three points.

What do you think? Is this information helpful?

Insurance Data Analytics for Digital Re-Imagination

Insurers can thrive in the dynamic markets of today through digital re-imagination. Differentiated and innovative offerings are backed by domain expertise and new-age technologies for accelerating performance and optimizing costs for growth with properties. They maintain and consolidate legacy systems that lead to moving towards digitalisation while monitoring regulatory compliance.

Adopting Insurance Analytics

In the world of increasing competition today, the changing risk profiles are calling for adoption of an insurance analytics solution for cost reduction and growth. The software service providers are using their technical capabilities and domain expertise to come up with digitally-driven solutions for greater industry value. They have offerings for streamlining operations to include system integration, configuration and customization, information management, product testing and application maintenance.

Data Conversion, Performance Measurement and Risk Analysis

Thereafter, a tool for automated data conversion can be sought to accelerate information transformation. Then, analytics and business performance measurement is required to improve distribution, manage customers and claim performance to measure Key Performance Indicators (KPIs). Then, proceed towards advanced risk analysis that can be applied to consolidate risk information.

Business Process and Regulatory Compliance

Reach out to the IT experts seeking business process services in policy, billing and claims to decrease manual intervention, enhance employee productivity and bring down the processing costs. Now, regulatory compliance and reporting is also necessary with the help of industry-proven services offered by skilled experts. Then, regression testing is automated to minimize system downtime when opted for business process testing.

Systematic Agile Approach to Digitalization

Thereafter, core claims, self-service portals and policy applications can be re-engineered through a systematic agile approach to development. The information insights are leveraged to connect and provide personalised customer experiences for better retention. Optimize operations and manage interactions to digitalize customers, vendors, channel partners and employees.

Improving Enterprise Outcomes Through Better Decisions

Now-a-days, leveraging big data is helping insurers to lower loss ratio, do risk pricing and make decision. It is possible to capture and mine dispersed unstructured and structured data through an insurance data analytics solution. It captures and does an analysis of information obtained from different sources for easy access to substantial data in real time. The solution offers analytics, both prescriptive and predictive to come to informed decisions and fetch better business outcomes.

Deriving Enterprising Benefits

Dashboards, reports and key performance indicators let you measure and monitor the KPIs across the value chain. You can derive many business benefits out of opting for insurance information analytics. They help you make an error-free selection while weighing profitable individual risks to derive revenue growth. It helps you in carrying out a profitable renewal business and enhances operational efficiency by giving timely insights into problems to reduce claims leakage.

How to Implement Big Data Analytics for Your Financial Firm

In this new age of enterprise computing, Big Data is not a choice anymore, it is becoming mandatory for many companies. With digital content rising rapidly, many businesses are using Big Data tools to stay up to date with the new technology.

Companies use data tools to analyze and contrast value from those huge data sets. They gain a competitive advantage, but it is only realized if data is processed intelligently, efficiently, and results are delivered in a swift manner.

Big Data analytics being generated in the financial industry must be analyzed. Processing this data quickly and intelligently could be worth up to billions of dollars, potentially. Investment firms and financial service companies use B.D in a variety of ways.

Banks and finance websites look at customer data so that they can develop custom products and services. The result is an increase in customer satisfaction. Analytics also help eliminate debt by treating each customer circumstances differently. This helps improve recovery rates, as well as eliminate recovery costs.

Payment platforms and firms use B.D capabilities to effectively detect fraudulent activity, transitioning from traditional sampling techniques to processing all transactions and in the process, quickly assessing all risks. Enterprises are using Big Data analytics to look at how their IT systems are performing and behaving, analyzing and indexing all data generated by the IT Infrastructure. That allows improved up-times and operational efficiencies.

Financial firms faced with increasing customer demands for improved and more services along with increased demands now have to deal with petabytes of data. Recognising that data is a serious corporate asset. There is an increased focus on data integrity with leaders in the business community wanting more consistency in information and regulators expressing doubts about the type of data that they will receive.

Most B.D developments today have traditional techniques to process the huge amount of data that must be processed. It is best for financial firms to divide everything into smaller tasks, which are then distributed through many different servers. Financial firms in the B.D market are likely going to go up because Big Data has a lot of potential that will greatly affect the market.

To increase speed and achieve **q**uicker results, Many financial firms are attempting to try a new concept. This concept will take small fragments of the B.D and process them using a server. This will increase the effectiveness of Big Data.

Frequently Asked Questions About Data Analytics

Lately, businesses seem to have woken up to the fact that data analytics (DA) can help them in determining the relevance of their existing models, and making informed decisions. Perhaps this explains why it is becoming increasingly popular; however, contrary to popular belief, it is yet to cause a stir. It is high time that a lot more businesses are made to unleash the potential of this science which can do wonders for their day-to-day operations. This can be done by increasing awareness, and clarifying the doubts, if any. The answers to the following questions would supposedly do the same, and clear the air once and for all:

What is it?

DA is a science; one that can help a business in examining raw data, and drawing conclusions from the same.

Is it the same as data mining?

Contrary to popular belief, data analytics is not the same as data mining; the former lays emphasis on inference while on the other hand, the latter focuses on sorting of data. Furthermore, unlike its counterpart, DA does not help a business in identifying undiscovered patterns. As a matter of fact, DA is all about deriving a conclusion; by and large, this derivation is done on the basis of the information that is already known to the researcher.

What purpose does it serve?

The prime purpose of this science is to analyze the data stored in a data warehouse, and derive some relevant conclusions which can be of some help to a business; however, DA serves more than one purpose. To begin with, it can be used for analyzing the website traffic and navigation patterns, and can help an online business in identifying the prospects. Believe it or not, even some of the banks and credit card companies have been using it to their advantage. Supposedly, these entities use DA to analyze the withdrawal and spending patterns, thereby doing their bit in preventing the fraudulent activities.

How has it changed the scenario?

Earlier, the businesses had no option but to pile up the information in a data warehouse; however, this often led to a cumbersome situation, wherein the businesses had to carry out a time-consuming process for finding out the answers to their *q*ueries. DA has made it possible for every business to examine its data, and draw up a conclusion in a timely manner. Furthermore, the businesses do not have to settle for less anymore; they can determine the efficiency of their existing systems or models, and phase out the redundant ones.

Conclusion

Thank you again for downloading this book!

I hope this book was able to help you to understanding the steps guide to Data analytics

Finally, if you enjoyed this book, then I'd like to ask you for a favor, would you be kind enough to leave a review for this book on Amazon? It'd be greatly appreciated!

Thank you and good luck!

I truly do appreciate it!

Best Wishes,

Lee Maxwell